Making Wine at Home the Professional Way

The Workbook

by

Lance Cutler

Copyright © 1996
by
Wine Patrol Press

Published by: Wine Patrol Press
P.O. Box 228
Vineburg, CA 95487
U.S.A.

FIRST WINE PATROL PRESS EDITION, MAY 1996

Copyright © 1996 by Lance Cutler
All rights reserved. No part of this work may be reproduced or transmitted in any form or by any means, electronic or mechanical, including photocopying and recording, or by any information storage or retrieval system without written permission of the author, except for the inclusion of brief quotations in a review.

Library of Congress Cataloging-in-Publication Data

Library of Congress Catalogue Number: 96-90038

Cutler, Lance. Making Wine at Home the Professional Way: The Workbook/ by Lance Cutler. --First Edition
p. cm
ISBN 0-9637438-3-X: $11.95 Softcover

Printed in the United States of America

For Sandy, who may not get an
early start, but is virtually impossible
to stop once she gets going.

ACKNOWLEDGMENTS

First and foremost, thanks to Lisa Weber. You can be my editor for as long as the muse moves me.

John Marsic who filmed and edited the video, and showed the patience of a saint, and Earl Blue who directed and talked up the whole project.

Bob Johnson and David Ogaz who did the cover treatments with a minimum of hassle and a maximum of professionalism.

Ron Zak, as always, the photographer.

Randy Baker at Vernal Productions for all the help and advice.

Thanks to all the people who gave advice, help and encouragement during the filming of the video and the writing of the workbook.

Thanks to each and every one of you who buy my books and videos for allowing me to fund the next project, which in this case is tequila. Heaven help us all.

CONTENTS

Chapter 1   Introduction   1
     How To Use This Book

Chapter 2   Winemaking Philosophy   4
     To Intrude or Not To Intrude
     • Consequences of Intruding

Chapter 3   Acquiring Grapes   7
     Use Freshly Picked Grapes • Make Sure the Grapes Are Ripe • Start with "Easy" Varieties • How Many Grapes Make a Bottle?

Chapter 4   Crushing and Fermenting   10
     Crushing Options • Sulfur Dioxide at the Crusher

Chapter 5   Adjusting the Must   12
     Sugar Additions • Lowering Sugar • Checking and Adjusting Acidity • Reducing Acid in Must • Yeast Selection • Fermentation Temperatures • Stages in Fermentation • Keeping Detailed Records

Chapter 6   Fermenting Red Wines   22
     Punching Down • Testing Daily • Pressing • Using Fermentation Locks • Malolactic Fermentation • Inoculating for Malolactic Fermentation

Chapter 7 Fermenting White Wines   27
   Pressing White Grapes • Settling and
   Racking • White Wine Fermentation
   • Pink Wines

Chapter 8 Finishing the Wines   31
   Finishing White Wines • Cold Stability
   • Heat Stability

Chapter 9 Oak Aging   34
   Why Use Oak? • Using Oak Wisely
   • Topping Barrels • Caring for Your Barrels

Chapter 10 Testing and Taking Notes   38
   Testing Your Wines • Taste is Most
   Reliable • The Tasting Regimen

Chapter 11 Using Sulfur Dioxide   41
   At the Crusher • Understanding Free
   and Total SO_2 • SO_2 Addition Chart
   • SO_2 Safety

Chapter 12 Cellar Demons   44
   Acetification • Oxidation • Hydrogen
   Sulfide H_2S • Molds and Yeasts • Too
   Much Oak • Stuck Fermentations

Chapter 13 Bottling   49
   Stability • Pre-bottling Measurements
   • Blending • Bottling

Glossary   53

1
INTRODUCTION

Imagine a long time ago in history, before refrigeration. Summer is over; the harvest is in. People have stored all kinds of fruit in the coolest depths of wherever they live. They are desperate to keep some of the summer's fruit with them through the hard winter.

One day, someone walking through this storage room bumps one of the earthen jars. The lid falls off. He looks into the jar, sees that the fruit has produced a juice that is bubbling away. He tastes the juice and finds it delightfully fruity, exactly reminiscent of fresh summer fruit. And yet, there is something else . . .

He tastes some more juice, and then a little more. Soon he finds himself higher than a kite, feeling euphoric, and about to take a nap.

Very likely, this is how wine was first invented. Fermentation, the natural conversion of grape sugar to alcohol, is the basic essence of winemaking. It's also a simple, natural occurrence. Nature, left to her own devices and given the right conditions, will make her own wine. Winemakers would do well to allow Mother Nature to follow her own course. We can help here and there and provide an amenable environment, but in the final analysis, all winemaking is a natural process.

How to Use This Book

Because winemaking is totally dependent upon Mother Nature and her cycles, all winemaking begins with the vines. Those vines go through annual periods of dormancy, budding, growth, and maturation. It makes no difference how eager, enthused, or talented the winemaker, if you're making wine from grapes, there is only one harvest per year. That being the case, it behooves a winemaker to study his or her winemaking chops before each harvest.

When I was winemaker for Gundlach Bundschu Winery, I would spend three or four days each year in early August sitting in a hammock. The hammock stretched between two giant oak trees nestled on a tiny beach next to our irrigation reservoir. Armed with a six-pack of cold beer and a stack of technical books, I would read about how to make wine each year to remind myself of all the details.

I advise you, the home winemaker, to do the same thing. The purpose of this workbook is to show you, step by step, how to best help Mother Nature turn fruit into wine. My 20 years of experience as a professional and home winemaker, along with my many years as a teacher, allow me to explain this process in simple, uncomplicated terms. This book will work best with my video, *Making Wine at Home the Professional Way with Lance Cutler*. The video will serve as a visual guide to winemaking, and demonstrate each step in the winemaking process. In the book, I have included more philosophy, detail, and options.

Together, the video and the book will help you make great wine, but they are not intended to be the final word on the subject. It will serve you well to use this book as a base, and to find other resources for more detailed information about winemaking. Your local library, your local wine shop, and several wine periodicals offer a wealth of information. Seek them out, read them, and add them to your lexicon of information. Here are a few books that I think will prove valuable to home winemakers, regardless of their level of competence:

- *Art of Making Wine* by Anderson Hull (1970, A Plume Book, 181 pages).

- *Home Winemaker's Handbook* by Walter Taylor and Richard Vine (1968, Harper & Row, 188 pages).

- *Making Table Wine at Home* by George Cooke and James Lapsley (1988, University of Davis, Division of Agriculture, 44 pages).

- *Modern Winemaking* by Philip Jackisch (1985, Cornell University Press, 289 pages).

Regardless of my years of experience, I am just beginning to understand the intricacies of the winemaking art. That complexity is the wonder of it—and in large part, what accounts for the magic in the bottle. While it's true that winemaking is a natural process, it's equally true that making wine is a complex, challenging art that's full of nuance and requires attention to detail.

So relax. Open a bottle of your favorite wine. Read through this book. Watch the video. Then take up the challenge: go out and make some wine for yourself. It's fun, rewarding, and delicious.

Lance Cutler
Sonoma, California

2
WINEMAKING PHILOSOPHY

Each vintage, before you start making wine, you need to develop a winemaking philosophy. Thinking about the type of wine you want to make ahead of time and then basing all your winemaking decisions on that philosophy will greatly contribute to better wines.

To Intrude or Not to Intrude

If you think of winemaking as a continuum from least intrusive to most intrusive, and learn the basic principles of each, then you can decide what you want to attempt as a winemaker. Let me explain using a lot of unfamiliar terms that you will learn as you read through this book.

The least intrusive way to make wine is to bring in the grapes, toss the whole bunches (stems and all) into your fermenter, crush them up a bit and let them ferment on their native yeasts. Once they start fermenting, punch them down by hand. Wait until the fermentation is over, then press, settle, and rack into your storage containers.

At the other end of the continuum, the most intrusive, you would pick the grapes, and crush and de-stem them into your fermenters. You would add sulfur dioxide (SO_2), let the must settle, and then add selected yeast and various yeast nutrients. You'd begin fermentation, control the temperature, and inoculate with a malolactic culture. You'd press the grapes, rack to your storage containers, and wait for malolactic fermentation to finish. Then you would adjust the SO_2 and acid levels, and filter the wine before bottling.

One way is not better than the other. They are simply ways of providing the same thing: a perfect environment for Mother Nature to turn grapes into wine.

Consequences of Intruding

If you try the *least* intrusive method, you would expect to get lots of fruit character, because of the whole berries. You would expect complexity from the native yeasts. You would expect tannin and flavors from the stems. You would plan on leaving the wine in barrels for at least two years in the hopes that it would finish malolactic fermentation on its own. If everything goes perfectly, you would end up with a completely natural wine, with no chemical additives. It would be intensely fruity, with delicate, complex flavors from the native yeast, and it would have a nice tannic structure because of the stems.

On the other hand, because you are using no SO_2 at the crusher, you run the risk of *lactobacillus* infection, which can make your wine taste like geranium leaves. Relying on a natural malolactic fermentation could lead to further *lactobacillus* infection, or to *pediococcus* infection and a burnt rubber hose taste. If the malolactic fermentation doesn't finish, the wine could turn cloudy and fizzy in the bottle. The stems in the fermenting juice may turn the wine bitter. If everything goes wrong (I believe this is known as Murphy's Law), you could end up with a bitter, fizzy wine that tastes and smells like something between geraniums and burnt rubber hoses, that occasionally pops corks and leaks all over your carpeting.

If everything works to perfection, the most intrusive method should provide a wine with good fruit because of the controlled temperature. It would be free of strange bacterial odors, because of the judicious use of

SO_2. The wine would ferment to dryness, and the malolactic fermentation would completely finish because of your selected yeast and starter. The wine should be free of bitterness, since no stems were used. In short, you'd end up with a stable wine, full of clean fruit flavors and balanced tannins that indicate great aging potential.

On the other hand, because you've used SO_2 early and often, you've wiped out the native yeasts. Relying solely on selected yeast strains could make your wine taste pretty one-dimensional. It would be free of bacterial odors, but since these same aromas, in minute amounts, add to a wine's complexity, your wine may be simple. Filtration may strip out much of the character of your wine. The end result could be a sound wine that is simply too boring to enjoy.

Now, don't get discouraged.

It is the purpose of this book to explain all the terminology that you don't understand. You can see that every time a winemaker attempts to achieve a winemaking goal, he risks sacrificing another winemaking goal. Most winemakers end up taking a middle road between the most intrusive and the least intrusive methods. As a first time winemaker, the more you can do to control your winemaking environment, the more likely you are to make superb wines.

Remember, winemaking is a natural process. If you start with good grapes, get a plan, keep everything sanitary and clean, keep all of your containers full, and do the work when it is required, chances are you'll have a very drinkable product. It will be something you'll be proud to share with friends. More than that, your friends will be glad to drink it, when it's offered.

3
ACQUIRING GRAPES

Use Freshly Picked Grapes

Since winemaking is a natural process, wine can be made from all kinds of fruits. Lovely wines can be made by the home winemaker using various fruits and the methodology described here. Likewise, very decent wines can be made from grape juice concentrate or frozen juice. But if you are striving to make great, age-worthy wine, then I believe you must begin with freshly picked grapes.

If you live close to a grape growing region, try calling the local vintner association. They will probably have a listing of member growers and the various grape varieties they have for sale. Some may be able to direct you to growers willing to sell small amounts to home winemakers. Realize that harvest is a time of great labor and tension for growers, and they may not be able to accommodate customers buying tiny amounts of grapes.

Home beer making and winemaking shops often buy modest amounts of grapes directly from growers for sale to their customers. Prices are slightly higher, but the grapes get delivered to the wine shop, and you don't have to hassle with the details. Be sure you have a full understanding of the charges, and try to get some quality guarantees regarding sugar levels and grape quality *before* you buy. Bear in mind that shipped grapes will not be as perfect as freshly picked grapes, but be sure you don't get stuck paying for underripe or very moldy grapes.

Make Sure the Grapes Are Ripe

The key to fine winemaking is starting with fully ripened grapes. In commercial production, the winemaker decides when the grapes are ready to be harvested using scientific markers like **degrees Brix** (° Brix) to measure sugar content, **pH** (a measure of acid versus alkalinity), and the **total acidity** of the grapes. Commercial winemakers also use sensory markers like taste. Home winemakers must select ripe grapes from those available from growers or those to be found at the local wine shops.

Ripe grapes usually have stems that are losing their greenness. The berries pull more easily from their stems. The seeds within the berry start to free up from the pulp and they begin to turn brown. The pulp of the berry softens, and the juice thickens slightly. Ripe grape juice should make your fingers sticky, and the grapes should taste ripe. Finally, they should be fully colored green, gold, or black.

If you can avoid it, don't buy grapes with broken skins or rotten fruit. These grapes can contain harmful molds, and may be filled with vinegar bacteria, which is the last thing any winemaker needs. Grapes in this condition will make unsound wine with all sorts of "off tastes." Of course, if the grapes you purchase have been shipped a long way, you will have to make concessions.

Start With "Easy" Varieties

The United States has a large number of recognized species of grapes. The two main wine families are *vinifera* and *labrusca*. *Labrusca* grapes, grown primarily in the eastern part of the United States, have very different aromas and flavors from the *vinifera* varieties. I have no practical experience with *labrusca* varieties, so be sure to ask your supplier which varieties are recommended for beginning winemakers.

Of the *vinifera* varieties, I recommend starting out with red varieties like zinfandel, cabernet sauvignon, or merlot. Red wines are easier to produce than white wines, because they are not as temperature dependent and they are more resistant to oxidation problems. When you're ready for more of a challenge, you can move on to pinot noir. Pinot noir is not more difficult to make than the others, but it's less consistent.

If you choose to make white wine, chardonnay is the one everyone drinks, but lovely wines can be made from gewürztraminer, riesling and sauvignon blanc, and you'll find the prices much cheaper.

How Many Grapes Make a Bottle?

Roughly speaking, the home winemaker can expect about 100–120 gallons of wine per ton from white wine varieties, and about 120–150 gallons per ton from red wine varieties. At home, where I only make red wines, I determine how much of any particular wine I want to make, and then I buy the corresponding amount of grapes.

If I want to make 30 gallons of zinfandel, I buy 500 pounds of zinfandel grapes. For a 15 gallon lot, I would buy 250 pounds of grapes. This usually gives me plenty of wine to fill my barrels, plus it gives me enough extra wine to keep my containers full as the wine evaporates.

Always talk to growers, shop owners, and experienced winemakers. Usually, they have much to tell you about grapes and winemaking, and usually they'll take the time to offer suggestions and advice.

4
CRUSHING AND FERMENTING

After you acquire your grapes, you should get them into your fermenters as soon as possible. It's best to work with cool fruit (50–60° F), so try to have your grapes picked in the morning. If the grapes are really hot, you might let them sit in boxes overnight if you live in an area with cool night time temperatures. Generally, the sooner you crush the grapes, the better.

Be sure you have cleaned and sanitized all equipment that might come into contact with the grapes. This includes the crusher, the fermenters, the hoses and even the grape boxes if possible. (A couple tablespoons of chlorinated trisodium phosphate (TSP) in a couple gallons of water make a good all-purpose cleaning solution.) **Be sure to rinse all of your treated equipment with plain water to clear any residual cleaning solution.**

Crushing Options

The simplest, least intrusive crushing method is to simply throw the grapes into the fermenters, stems and all. Then, using your hand, a two-by-four, or even your feet, crush some of the grapes. Sometime in the next two to four days the juice will start to ferment. I don't recommend this method, especially for first time winemakers, although it definitely saves you the hassle of buying or renting a crusher.

It's better, I think, to use a **stemmer/crusher** to separate the grapes from the stems and split the skins so the yeast can get to the juice. Many crushers have adjustable rollers, so you can determine how many whole berries will go into your fermenters. Whole berries tend to make a wine fruitier. More crushed berries tend to make a wine a bit more tannic. After the grapes have been destemmed and crushed, the resulting mass is called **must**.

Check the section on crushing in my video to see how to set up your crusher and the fermenters. New, sanitized 30-gallon plastic trash cans are inexpensive and make great fermenters. **Be sure to remember that once fermentation begins, you must allow room for the grapes to rise to the top of the container. For 30-gallon fermenters, leave a space of about 10–14 inches.**

One of the great advantages we home winemakers have over professionals is that we work with small amounts of grapes and have time to ensure that our fruit is clean. Regardless of your crushing method, be sure to remove leaves. If your grapes have any moldy or rotten berries, cut them out with a sharp pair of scissors. My rule is that if you can't or don't want to eat it, then it shouldn't go into your tank. It is tedious work, but it will greatly reward you with better wines.

Sulfur Dioxide (SO$_2$) at the Crusher

Especially for beginning winemakers, I recommend adding 30–60 **ppm** (parts per million) of **sulfur dioxide (SO$_2$)**. Sulfur dioxide is an antiseptic that inhibits bacterial growth and acts as an antioxidant. Adding SO$_2$ will slow down yeasts and may delay the onset of fermentation, but it will also inhibit any *lactobacillus* (a spoilage bacteria) in the must, and therefore is a sound practice to follow. To add the SO$_2$, check the chart in Chapter 10, dissolve the proper amount in a bit of warm water, and then add a little at a time as you crush the grapes. Mix thoroughly with the must.

5
ADJUSTING THE MUST

Basically, **fermentation** is the natural process where-by fruit sugars are turned into alcohol. The organism that makes this conversion possible is **yeast**. The yeast eats the sugar, and then converts it to alcohol and **carbon dioxide gas** (CO_2).

So, the first two decisions to make about fermentation are how much alcohol you want, and which yeast you want to perform the conversion. The amount of sugar present in your grapes will determine how much alcohol will end up in your wine. More importantly, the amount of sugar present in your grapes serves as an indicator of ripeness in those grapes. Grapes harvested at exactly the proper ripeness will almost always produce better wines than grapes harvested too early (underripe) or too late (overripe).

As an example, think of peaches. Underripe peaches tend to be hard and bitter with too much acidity and little or no aroma. Overripe peaches tend to be cloyingly sweet, with a heavy aroma, and a flat aftertaste. A perfectly ripe peach has a firm texture, beautifully aromatic fruit, a crisp sweetness, and a fresh fruit flavor. Grapes must be perfectly ripe if the wines made from those grapes are to have the most perfect flavor.

Getting grapes at exactly the right level of ripeness is the greatest challenge for the home winemaker. We measure the amount of sugar in grapes as **degrees Brix (°Brix).** We take those measurements using a **refractometer** or a **hydrometer**. These instruments can be purchased at your local wine shop. Most winemakers feel that grapes achieve optimum ripeness somewhere between 22.5–24.5° Brix. **Don't go by the numbers alone. Be sure to taste the grapes**. Often, taste will serve as your best guide to ripeness.

Sugar Additions

Unfortunately, no matter how hard you try, you may find yourself dealing with underripe or overripe fruit. In the case of underripe fruit, you may want to add some sugar, so that you at least end up with a wine that has a fair amount of alcohol.

With a few exceptions, wines with less than 12% alcohol tend to be too thin, and are more susceptible to bacterial problems. Use the table on the next page to make sugar additions if you deem them necessary. Dissolve granulated cane sugar (available from grocery stores) in a mixture of warm water and grape juice. Add to the must and mix well.

It is best to make sugar additions *before* the grapes start fermenting, but try not to make sugar additions on the day you crush the grapes. Often, especially with varieties like zinfandel which ripen unevenly, sugars *will go up* as the grapes sit overnight. This is caused by raisins slowly releasing sugar as they sit in the must. It is not uncommon for zinfandel to gain 1–3° Brix overnight. So be sure you have an accurate sugar reading *before* you make any adjustments.

A general caution about making any additions is to check and re-check your data. Be sure your measurements are accurate. Take them more than once, and take them over a period of time. Calculate your measurements, and check those calculations. Be sure you make any additions to the *correct* container. Accuracy, caution, and patience are essential when

making any type of addition. Mistakes during additions can irretrievably harm a good wine.

SUGAR ADDITIONS

Existing Brix	Add per gallon for 12% alcohol	Add per gallon for 13% alcohol	Add per gallon for 14% alcohol
16°	.58 lb./gal.	.68 lb./gal.	.78 lb./gal.
17	.49	.59	.69
18	.39	.49	.59
19	.30	.39	.50
20	.20	.30	.40
21	.10	.20	.30
22	0	.10	.20
23	0	0	.10
24	0	0	.05

NOTE: 1° Brix produces approximately 0.575 percent alcohol.

Lowering Sugar

When grapes come into your winery with too much sugar, you have a couple of ways to go. The problem with high sugar is that the yeasts are piggish. They will keep eating the sugar, and keep turning the sugar into alcohol. Unfortunately, when the alcohol approaches 16%, it actually starts killing the yeast. If the yeast haven't finished eating all the sugar, you will be left with a wine that is both high in alcohol *and* sweet. These wines are called late harvest wines, and can be delicious, but usually are not. They also present a stability problem for the home winemaker, because after the wine is bottled (unless you sterile filter) some dormant yeasts can wake up, start eating the residual sugar, produce CO_2, and pop the corks right out of your bottles.

If you decide late harvest wines are not for you, you can lower the sweetness of the juice with water. It is best to add about two tablespoons of tartaric acid *per gallon* of water before adding it to the must. Use this formula to determine how much water to use.

WATER ADDITIONS

$$\frac{A \times B}{C} - B = D$$

A = ° Brix
B = Number of gallons
C = Desired ° Brix
D = Gallons of water to add

Multiply ° Brix (A) times the number of gallons of juice (B). Then divide by the desired ° Brix (C) and subtract the number of gallons you started with (B) to find how much water to add (D). For example, let's say you have 30 gallons of zinfandel at 26° Brix. You decide to reduce the sugar to 24.5° Brix. This will result in a powerful, alcoholic wine that should ferment to dryness. Multiply ° Brix (26) times the number of gallons of juice (30), and then divide by the desired ° Brix (24.5).

26 x 30 = 780
780 ÷ 24.5 = 31.8 gallons
31.8 - 30 = 1.8 gallons

You need to add 1.8 gallons of water to the 30 gallons of juice to lower the sugar from 26° Brix to 24.5° Brix.

Checking and Adjusting Acidity

Grapes naturally contain several different acids. The most common is **tartaric acid**; the next most frequently found is **malic acid** (which in most cases is converted finally to **lactic acid**). Wines with low acid tend to be flat, uninteresting, and have a dull aftertaste. Low acid wines won't ferment well, will be harder to clarify, and are more susceptible to bacterial problems. High acid wines are bright with fruit, but will always remain tart and unyielding.

Testing for acid in juice and wines is tricky. See Chapter 11 for testing ideas. More often than not, especially in California, you will encounter low acids rather than high ones. I recommend making all acid additions with tartaric acid. After all, tartaric is what the grapes have produced themselves. Use the table below to make an acid addition.

ACID ADDITIONS

Present acid	Add per gallon for .70	Add per gallon for .80	Add per 5 gallons for .70	Add per 5 gallons for .80
.500	7.6 grams	11.4 grams	37.8 grams	56.7 grams
.550	5.7	9.5	28.4	47.2
.600	3.8	7.6	18.9	37.8
.650	1.9	5.7	9.5	28.4
.700	0.0	3.8	0.0	18.9
.750	0.0	1.9	0.0	9.5

Tartaric Acid

Rough equivalents:
1/4 tsp. = 1.3 grams   1 tsp. = 5.5 grams
1/2 tsp. = 2.7 grams   1 tbs. = 16.5 grams

Dissolve the tartaric acid in a small amount of warm water, pour the liquid into the must, and mix thoroughly. The acid will slowly work its way into the must, so don't panic if tests show high acids for the next 12–36 hours.

Reducing Acidity in Must

If your must tests higher than 1.0 total acid, you can reduce acidity by adding water to the must. When adding water, you should never add more than 15% of the volume of the juice. In fact, I try not to add water at all, because I suspect it dilutes the flavor intensity of my juice. However, remember it is always better to add water to juice than to finished wine.

Multiply the number of gallons of must (B) by the acid level (A). Divide the result by the acid level you hope to achieve (C). The result is (D). Subtract B from D to determine how many gallons of water to add.

Let's say you have 20 gallons of must (B) and the acid is 1.0 (A). You decide to lower it to .90 (C). Multiply the number of gallons (20) times the acid (1.0). That gives you a total of 20. Divide that number by .90. Take the result, 22.2 gallons (D), then subtract the original gallons. You would need to add 2.2 gallons of water to 20 gallons of must to lower the acid level from 1.0 to .90.

LOWERING ACIDITY

$$\frac{A \times B}{C} - B = D$$

A = Acid level
B = Number of gallons
C = Desired acid level
D = Gallons of water to add

Yeast Selection

Assuming that you have perfectly ripe grapes, or that you have adjusted the sugar to the desired level, your next decision deals with yeast selection. Dozens of yeast strains have been developed for winemakers. Each gives some specific advantage (like low foaming *prix de mousse* for use in barrel fermentation). You will get the best information by talking to your local wine shop representative or to the yeast producers themselves. Tell them which grapes you are using, what style you are attempting, and at what temperature you are fermenting the wine.

Yeast comes with simple instructions that tell you to mix a certain amount in warm water, wait a period of time, and then add to the must. It is best to follow the directions, but it will probably also work if you just dump some yeast directly into the must, wait a few hours, and then mix it up. More and more winemakers are adding yeast nutrients to the must before fermentation. In many cases, nutrients are unnecessary, but you might want to discuss them with your local wine shop expert.

I think it best for beginning winemakers to use commercially prepared yeasts, especially the first few times. Later if you want to try something a little riskier that may add complexity to your wines, you can try fermenting with **native yeasts** that exist naturally on the grapes. To conduct a fermentation with native yeasts, you would use little or no SO_2 at the crusher, and wait longer for the fermentation to start.

Fermentation Temperatures

Simply put, the law of fermentation states that the cooler the fermentation temperature, the fruitier the wine. A hotter fermentation results in a more complex wine. The catch is that you can't have it both ways. To achieve one, you must sacrifice some of the other.

Wines like gewürztraminer and riesling, whose greatest charms lie in their fruity character, are fermented at very cool temperatures (50–55° F). Chardonnay and sauvignon blanc, which are prized for their fruity character as well as their ability to carry more complex flavors, are fermented in the 55–70° F range. Red wines are meant to be the most complex, so they are fermented the hottest, usually between 75–90° F. Accurately controlling temperature during fermentation is a key winemaking decision, and will influence the style of the finished wine as much as anything the winemaker does.

Test and record the sugar level and temperature of the must at least twice a day during fermentation. Note that during fermentation ° Brix is known as ° **Balling**. In my video, I recommend using a hydrometer that contains a thermometer, so you can check temperatures at the same time you check sugar levels. It may be necessary to quickly cool down fermenting must, so keep a few two-liter plastic soda or juice bottles filled with water in the freezer, and submerge them into the must until the temperature drops. To prepare the bottles, strip the labels, wash the bottles, fill them with water, cap them, and stick them in the freezer. **Be sure the caps are tight, so water doesn't leak into your juice.**

Stages of Fermentation

At the beginning of fermentation, yeast cells grow and increase in number so they can begin active fermentation. Depending on the yeast and the temperature of the must, it takes between 12 hours and 3–5 days to begin active fermentation. Native yeasts will usually take longer than commercial yeasts.

During vigorous fermentation, the yeast is most active, consuming huge amounts of sugar and converting the sugar to alcohol. This creates lots of heat and CO_2 gas. White wines will tend to froth. Red wines will froth, and the skins will rise to the surface and form a cap that should be forced back into the juice on a regular basis.

As fermentation winds down, the yeast becomes less active, and conversion continues at a much slower rate. The must will cool quite a bit. In white wines, the frothy top will dry out and may turn brown. In red wines, the cap of grape skins may sink down into the liquid.

At some point you need to make sure that all fermentable sugars have been used up. You can get a fairly accurate indication by using pills that test the sugar content of liquid. These are often used by diabetics to monitor their sugar levels and are available in pharmacies, as well as winemaking shops.

Keeping Detailed Records

Complete, accurate record keeping is vital if you want to make great wine. See the sample Crush Notes on the next page for an example of the notes I keep. At the very least, you should record the following:
- At harvest, record the date of harvest, the grape variety, ° Brix, total acidity, and pH.
- As you are crushing the grapes, note any SO_2, acid or sugar additions, and make notes about smells, textures, and visual observations.
- During fermentation, record ° Balling and temperature twice daily. Note activity and odors.
- Write down each transfer and note any additions. Taste the wine often and write down your impressions of the bouquet, finish and flavor of the wine.

CRUSH NOTES

Variety Pinot Noir   **Vineyard** Neighbor's

Harvest Date 9-20-96 **Brix** 23.9 **pH** 3.40 **TA** .80

Date	Temp	°Balling	Notes & Additions
9/20	62°	23.9°	Crush, add 30 ppm SO_2
9/21	66	23.9	Punch down (PD), add yeast
9/21	66	23.9	PD noon, 5 p.m., 10 p.m.
9/22	67	23.9	PD 8 a.m., 1 p.m.
9/23	70	23.0	Active fermentation, PD 8 a.m.
9/23	74	23.0	PD noon, 4 p.m., 8 p.m.
9/24	80	22.0	PD 8 a.m., noon
9/24	88	16.5	PD 4 p.m., 8 p.m.
9/25	88	12.0	PD 8 a.m., noon, skunky smell
9/25	86	8.0	PD 5 p.m., 10 p.m.
9/26	80	5.5	PD 8 a.m., noon
9/26	80	3.0	PD 5 p.m., 10 p.m.
9/27	76	1.0	PD 8 a.m., no skunky smells
9/27	74	0.0	PD 4 p.m., 10 p.m.
9/28	72	-0.5	PD noon, add ML starter
9/28	72	-1.0	PD 6 p.m.
9/29	70	-1.0	PD 8 a.m., noon
9/29	70	-1.5	PD 5 p.m.
9/30	70	-1.8	Press to carboys (36 gallons)

6
FERMENTING RED WINES

Fermenting red wines is a pretty straightforward process. After crushing the grapes into your **fermenters** (containers in which you ferment the grapes), using the SO_2 regimen you've selected, and waiting for your yeast to get going, your main job is **punching down**.

Be sure to cover your fermenters with a clean cloth to keep fruit flies and other critters out of the juice.

Punching Down

As red wine starts to ferment, the grape skins rise to the top and form a cap. Because most of the flavor and color components are stored in the skins, it is important that these skins be pushed back into the juice. Also, because the conversion of sugar to alcohol generates a lot of heat, punching down helps cool the temperature of the must and allows you to better control fermentation temperatures.

You can buy or make tools for punching down, but the cheapest, most efficient tool is your arm. Simply push the grapes back into the liquid. In the beginning, the grapes will be swimming in the juice, and you can use your arm like a giant stirrer. As the fermentation turns vigorous, use your hand to push a hole through the cap in the middle of the fermenter, then work your way around the fermenter until all of the grapes are submerged. As the fermentation finishes, the spent skins will slowly sink back into the juice. At this point you can return to the stirring motion.

You should begin punching down the day you crush the grapes. A minimum of two to three punch downs a day is recommended. I increase the amount of punch downs to five or six per day during vigorous fermentation, and then return to two or three times daily at the end. As I have said, any tool will work, but using your arm will give you a real feel for each grape variety and each fermenter. You will readily understand the stages of fermentation. You will *feel* the temperature rise, as well as the difference in temperature between the cap and the juice.

Testing Daily

It is essential that you use your hydrometer and thermometer to record temperature and ° Balling at least daily. This process is shown in my video. It simply involves filling a cylinder with juice, dropping in the hydrometer, and reading the proper scale. Recording the information daily (see the Crush Notes in Chapter 5) gives you a written guide that will become part of your experiential expertise. It will let you know when fermentation actively begins, when it peaks, and when it finishes. It will alert you to a **stuck fermentation** (a fermentation that stops before all the sugar has been converted to alcohol), so you can warm the must or add nutrients to get it moving again.

Pressing

Deciding when to press a vat of red wine is as often a matter of convenience as any other factor. Most home winemakers have to do their work on weekends. They often pick the grapes one weekend and press the next weekend. Research shows that most of the flavor is extracted from the skins in the first three to five days, so pressing any time after is acceptable. That said, leaving skins in contact with the juice for a longer period of time can greatly increase the complexity and body of a red wine. Given the opportunity I like to press 10–14 days after crushing.

Describing a press and how to actually press a tank of grapes is difficult. This is where my video *Making Wine at Home the Professional Way* can really help you make wine, because you can actually watch me go through the whole process. Basically, a press involves some sort of basket which sits on a base. You fill the basket with the must, and the juice runs out through the holes or gaps in the basket. When the basket is full of grapes, you press down on the grapes to extract more juice. As the wine pours from the press, use a strainer with small holes to catch grapes, seeds, and heavy sediment, known as **lees**. An ordinary kitchen strainer works well.

Juice that runs through the press of its own accord is **free run juice**. Juice that comes out while you are squeezing the grapes is called **press juice**. Free run juice tends to be fruitier, more acidic, and less tannic than the press juice. Press juice is usually less fruity, less acidic, more tannic, and more full-bodied than free run juice. Most winemakers combine the free run with the press juice. I recommend that you keep them separate and taste them individually, so you can learn the distinctions. Then you can make your own decisions about whether to combine them.

Using Fermentation Locks

After pressing, the wine is likely to continue fermenting for a while. When you move or **rack** the wine to barrels or glass containers known as **carboys**, be sure to use fermentation locks to seal those containers. **Fermentation locks** are devices that allow CO_2 gas to escape and prevent air from entering a container. Simple plastic fermentation locks are inexpensive and readily available at local wine shops.

Malolactic Fermentation

In addition to the primary fermentation, when sugar is converted to alcohol and CO_2 gas, red wines (and some chardonnays) should undergo a secondary fermentation known as **malolactic fermentation**. This fermentation occurs when bacteria consume the malic acid naturally found in grapes and change it to lactic acid and CO_2 gas.

We want malolactic fermentation to occur for two reasons. First, **malic acid** is the acid found in green apples, while **lactic acid** is the acid found in milk and cheese. When the malolactic fermentation converts the stronger malic acid into the less harsh lactic acid, the wine becomes less harsh as well. Second, in home winemaking situations where we usually use no filtration, malolactic fermentation must be completed to assure stability of the bottled wine. If malolactic is not complete, and you bottle the wine, you run the risk of the malolactic fermentation starting up in the bottle. If this happens the wine will turn cloudy, throw a sediment, and the buildup of CO_2 gas could cause the wine to leak through the corks, or even make the corks shoot out of the bottles.

Inoculating for Malolactic Fermentation

Malolactic fermentations are carried out by bacteria. Often these bacteria are present on the grapes themselves or in the barrels in which the wines are stored. Because certain bacteria can produce some pretty strange tastes and flavors, most winemakers inoculate with a prepared malolactic bacteria. We use a strain called

leuconostoc oenus. Most convenient for home winemakers is a freeze dried strain of *leuconostoc oenus* that can be added directly to the must or the wine. You can purchase this bacteria from most home winemaking shops.

Malolactic bacteria are fickle creatures that require a hospitable environment to do their work. They flourish while the wine is kept in contact with the lees (heavy sediment). They also prefer higher pH (above 3.3), warm temperatures (above 60° F), and they hate SO_2. You can track malolactic fermentations by using **paper chromatography**, a simple test that requires no special skills, and can be purchased at your local winemaking shop.

7
FERMENTING WHITE WINES

Making white wine is more difficult than making red wine, because white wine is more susceptible to oxidation and browning. Also, because white wines are fermented at much cooler temperatures than red wines (to retain their fruity flavors and aromas), refrigeration is necessary.

Pressing White Grapes

White grapes should be crushed, pressed, and then settled before fermentation. Crush the grapes just as you would for red wine. Put the crushed grapes into the press. Because you are pressing grapes instead of fermented grape skins, the must will be slippery and will want to squirt out between the slats on your press. You can help prevent this by placing stems in the bottom, top, and in the slot openings of your basket press. Pressing unfermented white grapes will yield less juice than pressing fermented red grapes. (See Chapter 3 for estimated juice yields.)

Settling and Racking

The best white wines are made from juice that has been settled and racked after being pressed. **Settling** means to allow the sediment to form in the bottom of its container. Later, you will **rack** or siphon off the clear juice into a new container. When fermented, the clear juice, will exhibit fruitier aromas and flavors than wine made from unsettled juice which tends to be bitter, ponderous, and lacking in fruit.

To settle white juice, pour the juice into a container avoiding as much splashing and oxygenation as possible. Be sure that the containers are **topped up** (filled to the top leaving no air space). If possible, keep the free run juice separate from the press juice, and keep settling juice cold (less than 50° F) to help prevent the start of fermentation. At home, I've found that five gallon glass carboys are convenient. I can fit two of them into an old refrigerator, and it's easy to see when the settled wine has separated from the lees.

It is essential that your settling juice does *not* start fermenting. If fermentation occurs at this stage, then all the solids become involved and you will be unable to separate them. In addition to keeping the juice cold, be sure to add 30–60 ppm of SO_2 to the settling juice. It's easier to make accurate additions to the pressed juice than to the must before pressing.

After the juice has settled (usually 24 hours, but it can take longer), you should rack the clear juice off the lees into another container. You should readily see where the clear juice has separated from the lees. Be sure to keep only the clear juice. Expect to lose 10–15% of the settled juice to lees.

White Wine Fermentation

Having racked the juice to your fermenter, you are ready to add yeast. **Be sure your fermenter is no more than three-quarters full to allow for foaming during fermentation.** Since fermentation will generate CO_2 gas, chances of wine oxidation are minimal. Be sure to use a fermentation lock. If wine foams up into the lock, be diligent about cleaning it.

As with red wine, you should check temperature and ° Balling often. If you're fermenting in glass carboys, you will be able to see that the wine is fermenting, and can check ° Balling less often (once every two or three days).

Because you are fermenting at cooler temperatures, white wine fermentations take longer than red wine fermentations, usually 2–3 weeks.

Once fermentation is completed, top up the fermenters, secure the fermentation locks, and allow the sediment to settle to the bottom. Keep the wine cold (between 55–60° F). When the wine clears, rack to another clean container, and adjust the SO_2. Be sure to top the container.

Because white wines are fermented and stored at colder temperatures, they tend to absorb some CO_2. For this reason, it is a good idea to keep fermentation locks on white wine containers. That way, if the wine warms up, and the CO_2 is released, the gas has a way to escape.

Pink Wines

Pink wines are made from red grapes which are handled as if you were making white wine. Crush and press the red grapes as described for white wine production. Settle the juice, rack, add the yeast, and ferment at cool temperatures. Rack again and keep the containers topped up. Dry pink wines can be enchanting, especially in the spring.

Unfortunately, most people like pink wines because they are sweet. Bottling sweet wines safely for the home winemaker is very risky. Because home winemakers can rarely achieve sterile bottling, their wine will likely contain some yeast cells. Sweet wines contain sugar, which is food for yeast. Sooner or later, those yeast cells will get hungry and start eating the sugar. This will produce additional alcohol and CO_2 gas, which will likely pop corks.

I don't recommend bottling sweet wines at home, but if you must, try renting a filter from your local wine shop, and attempt a sterile bottling. Keep SO_2 levels up, and be sure to keep the bottled wine refrigerated. That may keep the yeast too cold and weak to get hungry.

8
FINISHING THE WINES

Once wine has finished fermenting, it becomes susceptible to a host of maladies, all of which can cause it to taste or smell awful. Keeping all equipment clean, sanitizing hoses, using proper amounts of SO_2, and keeping containers topped up will help protect your wine.

Finishing White Wines

New white wines should be kept cool, about 60° F if possible. Racking them every 4–6 weeks will help clarify the wine, and will allow you to taste the wine at regular intervals. Remember that wine must be protected from oxygen. **Be sure to keep your racking hose in the bottom of any new container to limit the amount of splashing during any rackings. The less oxidation, the better in white winemaking.** It's also a good idea to keep the container sealed with a fermentation lock in case there is any residual CO_2

Cold Stability

Regular racking will help clarify white wines, but both red and white wines can still have some stability problems. White wines naturally contain quite a bit of tartaric acid and small levels of potassium. When wines are chilled, either in the refrigerator or in a cold wine cellar, the tartaric acid and the potassium combine to form **potassium bitartrate**. This natural precipitate forms crystals, which most likely will stick to the cork, or form in the bottom of the bottle. These **tartrates** are harmless, but they are gritty, so they can be unpleasant. In white wines the crystals look like bits of glass, and can seriously freak out a novice wine drinker.

Usually, wines that are kept in containers through a cold winter before being bottled will throw tartrates on their own, but both red wines and white wines can be cold stabilized by chilling the wines to 32–38° F for 2–4 weeks before bottling the wine. In either case the tartrates will form in the carboy or barrel. The wine can be racked clear of the tartrates, and the finished wine should remain free of crystals even when chilled.

Heat Stability

White wines also have a heat stability problem. When the wines are exposed to high temperatures, such as the trunk of your car or your living room wine rack during the summer, proteins will precipitate from the wine and make it cloudy. Once again, this is a harmless, natural occurrence, but it is unattractive.

Heat stability of white wines is tricky. Basically, before bottling the wine you must add **bentonite** (a special type of clay). The bentonite will link up with the proteins and drag them to the bottom of the container. The wine can then be racked off the lees. The problem is that protein stability is pH dependent. The amount of bentonite you need to use changes according to the pH and is different for each wine.

Using bentonite can be harsh treatment for a delicate white wine. Many wineries now add bentonite to settling juice *before* fermentation. The juice is tougher than wine, and seems to better stand up to bentonite treatment.

If you insist on heat stability in your white wines, be sure to ask about the procedure at your local wine shop. **At the very least consult other books to get a**

more detailed explanation of the procedure. Fortunately, red wines contain natural compounds that make them heat stable, so they require no additional treatment.

Remember, both red and white wines need to be cold stabilized. Only white wines require heat stability treatment. Personally, I don't make white wines at home, so I don't worry about heat stability. And if the cold winter doesn't completely cold stabilize my red wines, I choose not to worry about the few tartrates that form on the cork.

9
OAK AGING

Only the quality of your grapes and carefully controlled fermentation temperatures influence the flavor of your finished wine more than your choice of oak. In my opinion, **the most common problem among both professional and home winemakers is that they use too much oak.**

Why Use Oak?

There are two reasons to use oak in winemaking. First is flavor. Oak seems to enhance the flavor of wine, especially red wines and chardonnay. Used this way, oak is to winemaking what garlic is to cooking. The proper amount enhances and adds complexity. Too much overpowers and ultimately diminishes. Of course, determining "the proper amount" is strictly a personal matter.

The second reason for using oak is more complicated. Wines aged in oak barrels tend to taste smoother and richer than the same wines kept in glass carboys or stainless steel tanks. The exact reasons for this are a bit of a mystery. Perhaps small amounts of oxygen find their way into the wine and help with the aging process. Whatever the cause, wines aged in oak barrels tend to be more complex and interesting than wines that have not.

Using Oak Wisely

This whole question of oak aging is very difficult for the home winemaker. First of all, oak barrels are expensive, approximately $6–$8 per gallon! Second, small oak barrels often impart too much oak flavor into a wine. Third, it is a *very bad* idea to leave barrels empty for any length of time, because bacteria will likely grow inside the barrel.

If you are making a small batch of wine, less than 60 gallons, you will find it easier to use oak chips or a similar product instead of barrels. Oak chips are an inexpensive way to give your wine oaky aromas and flavors, but don't expect the mysterious complexity of wines aged in oak barrels. Do *not* cut up some oak you have lying around the garage to put in your wine. Properly prepared, toasted oak chips are available at most home winemaking shops, and are easy to order directly from producers if unavailable in your area. When using oak chips, taste the wine often, because they tend to impart lots of flavor very quickly.

When you are working with 60 gallons or more, barrels will certainly contribute to better wines. The key is to protect yourself from giving your wines too much oak flavor. You also want to keep your barrels full at all times. If you plan to buy new barrels, buy enough to hold 25–35% of your total production. For example, let's say that you made 60 gallons of zinfandel. Buy one 15-gallon oak barrel. Fill the barrel with cold water until it swells and stops leaking. Then empty the barrel and fill with wine. Keep the rest of your wine in carboys or stainless steel containers. The first wine into the barrel will extract oak flavors very quickly, so taste often. When the wine has the amount of oak flavoring you like, rack the wine to carboys. Then put another 15 gallons into the barrel. When that wine tastes right, rack it to carboys, and fill the barrel again.

You will find that the first batch in the barrel gets oaky quickly, probably 4–6 weeks. The second batch may take 8–12 weeks to achieve the desired level of oak flavor.

Using this method, you can minimize the amount you need to spend on barrels, get more control over the amount of oak you impart to the wines, and you keep the barrel full. **One final word of caution:** *never* **buy a used barrel.** If used barrels contain harmful bacteria, you won't know it until they've affected your wine. New barrels cost more, but in the long run they are cheaper, because they are less likely to infect your wine.

Topping Barrels

As with any container during the wine process, it is critical to keep your barrels topped up. Wine evaporates from oak barrels. Be sure to top your barrels at least once or twice *every* month. Taste the wine at least once a month to monitor its development, and to assess the amount of oak flavor it is picking up. Try to describe what you are tasting, and write it down. Over time, these written notes will provide valuable information for future winemaking projects.

As your barrels get older, they will impart less and less oak flavor. Wines will need to stay in the barrels for longer periods of time. Especially in the case of red wines, racking every two to three months will help clarify the wine. The gentle oxidation that occurs during racking will contribute to a softer, more full bodied wine.

Caring for Your Barrels

Be sure to rinse your barrels with clean water every time you empty them. If, in spite of your best efforts, you must store an empty barrel, fill it with a 200 ppm solution of SO_2 and some tartaric acid, bung the barrel, and let it sit for up to a month. If you must store the barrel longer, try burning sulfur sticks (available at most wine shops) inside your empty barrels at recommended intervals. Take care of your barrels. They can greatly improve your wines, but neglected they can easily become a major source of bacteriological contamination

10
TESTING AND NOTE TAKING

Cleanliness is certainly the number one responsibility of any good winemaker, but it is absolutely essential that winemakers take notes throughout the winemaking process. You should record all data regarding the grapes themselves, the fermentation process, additions of any kind, all pertinent test data, and all sensory evaluation. Diligent record keeping will help prevent you from making mistakes like adding acid to the same wine more than once or forgetting to add SO_2 to wine after malolactic fermentation.

It is also helpful to look back on your notes each subsequent vintage to see if there is anything to be learned, especially when you are working with grapes from the same vineyard year after year. Notes will remind you how certain grapes reacted to rainy vintages or extremely hot growing seasons. This is valuable information that allows you to anticipate vintage related problems.

Testing Your Wines

My background is in home winemaking. I was not trained to be a winemaker. I did not go to a school of Enology to learn my trade. I am definitely a hands-on winemaker with a great appreciation for old world methods. That said, I still think a few basic lab tests are essential to making good wine.

At the bare minimum, you should know the sugar content (° Brix), the pH, and the total acidity (TA) of your grapes. You should track the pH, the TA and the SO_2 levels of your finished wines. Take these measurements regularly, especially after fermentation, after malolactic fermentation, after racking, and before bottling.

All of these tests involve some basic knowledge of chemistry, but nothing too complicated for a home winemaker. Unfortunately, the equipment required to accurately run these tests can be prohibitively expensive. Frankly, affordable equipment for home winemakers is just not accurate. You can have these tests run at any chemistry lab, which will not be cheap, but will be less expensive than purchasing top notch equipment.

I think a better idea is to go to your local high school or junior college, and hire a good chemistry student to run the tests for you. This is winemaking at its best. You get the opportunity to meet a new friend. You educate someone about the joys of wine and winemaking. A student gets some much needed cash, and you should get accurate test results for minimum cost.

Tasting Is Most Reliable

Once you get access to test information, don't turn into a lab geek. Test results provide good information, and you can use that information to guide you in winemaking decisions. But it is just as important to rely on your own judgment. Taste the wines, make your assessments, and use the test data as a backup.

For example, if your wine has a strange, soapy taste and seems flat, it probably has a high pH and needs some acid. Now, check your test results and see if they confirm your evaluation. If the pH is 4.00, and the TA is .53, then you are assured that a modest acid addition will lower the pH, reduce the soapy taste, and brighten the finish of the wine.

Test data can indicate possible problem areas. High pH and low acid can lead to bacterial problems, while high acid and low pH can prevent malolactic fermentation. **Before you make any additions or corrections, taste the wine**, think about the consequences of what you are doing, and decide if it is absolutely necessary. Then scale down the treatment and try it on a small sample *before* trying it on the whole batch.

The Tasting Regimen

Tasting your wines regularly is important for any winemaker, and it's the most fun. I try to taste each of my wines at least twice a month: I make notes of the various aromas and tastes. I try to record the sensation in my mouth as well as the aftertaste. I pay close attention to the oak levels in both the **bouquet** (smells in the wine due to winemaking) and the flavor of the wine.

Be aware that wine is a living substance. It can change in flavor drastically from week to week. Patience is a virtue in winemaking. Only experience can teach the home winemaker how to distinguish the normal changes in aroma and taste of a young developing wine, from more serious problems. That is why conscientious note taking is so valuable.

11
USING SULFUR DIOXIDE

Sulfur dioxide (SO_2) prevents the growth of undesirable yeast and bacteria; it also can help prevent oxidation. It is extremely effective in minute amounts, usually a few parts per million (ppm). Its effectiveness is related to the pH of the wine. It is more potent at lower pH and less potent at higher pH. After cleanliness, SO_2 is the winemaker's most effective tool in controlling unwanted bacterial growth.

At the Crusher

Wine is most at risk before fermentation and after fermentation is completed. During fermentation, wine is protected by all the CO_2 gas generated during the conversion from sugar to alcohol. Using SO_2 at the crusher is generally a good idea. Somewhere between 30–60 ppm will help prevent growth of unwanted bacteria and yeast. After fermentation (including malolactic fermentation), proper SO_2 additions will protect and stabilize the wine.

Understanding Free and Total SO_2

SO_2 reacts quickly with other compounds found in wine. Portions of SO_2 quickly become **bound** to these other compounds, while the rest of the SO_2 remains **free**. *Only the free SO_2 is effective as an anti-bacterial agent.* We measure SO_2 in both its free and its total state. **Total SO_2** includes the free and the bound SO_2. Use the following chart as a guide for free SO_2 in your finished wines.

IDEAL FREE SO_2 LEVELS

pH	White Wines	Red Wines
3.00	13 ppm	8 ppm
3.10	16	10
3.20	21	13
3.30	26	16
3.40	32	20
3.50	40	25
3.60	50	31
3.70	63	39
3.80	79	49
3.90	99	62
4.00	125	78

Rough Equivalents: 1 gram SO_2 = 150 ppm in 1 gallon
1 gram SO_2 = 30 ppm in 5 gallons

1/4 tsp. = 1.3 g.   1/2 tsp. = 2.7 g.   1 tsp. = 5.5 g.

Finished white wines generally require *more* free SO_2 to achieve the same anti-bacterial effectiveness as red wines. As evidenced by the chart, the effectiveness of SO_2 is pH dependent. SO_2 is recommended for all wines. Add SO_2 when crushing, after malolactic fermentation and before bottling (based on pH levels). If possible, maintain the SO_2 levels indicated on the chart. You will find it virtually impossible to maintain proper SO_2 levels above 3.7 pH. As a winemaker, you have two choices: make an acid addition to lower pH, or leave less SO_2 and hope for the best. The safest bet, if the acid addition won't mess up the wine, is to make the addition, and then adjust the SO_2 levels accordingly.

SO_2 Safety

SO_2 is a great friend to the winemaker, but the very qualities that make it such an effective anti-bacteriological agent demand that we treat it with respect. When working with SO_2, try not to breathe in any of the dust. Avoid, as much as possible, contact with the skin. Should you swallow some SO_2 solution or get some in your eyes, flush with water and get yourself to a doctor. If you use common sense, you will have no problems with SO_2, but be aware that in case of an accident it behooves you to get prompt proper treatment.

12
CELLAR DEMONS

Most winemaking problems can be prevented. First and foremost, things must be sanitary and clean. Second, wines should be made from fresh, ripe grapes. Third, all containers holding wine must be kept topped up. Fortunately, because wine contains alcohol and has a relatively low pH, nothing terribly harmful to humans can live in wine. That said, there are a host of things that can grow in wine to make it taste or smell lousy.

Acetification

The biggest worry for the home winemaker is the problem of **acetification,** or vinegar formation. Acetification is caused by acetic acid bacteria found in moldy, damaged, or overripe grapes. These bacteria can also be introduced by the tiny fruit flies that tend to hover around fermenting wines. The bacteria need air or oxygen and a weak alcohol solution to make vinegar. Acetification turns the wine into **acetic acid,** which has a vinegary smell or **ethyl acetate,** which smells like nail polish remover.

If you keep your equipment clean, use sound, ripe grapes, use sulfur dioxide, ferment to at least 12% alcohol, and keep your containers topped up, you should have no problems with acetification.

If your wine becomes acetified, you have two choices: throw it away or decide to make vinegar. Under no circumstances should you put acetified wine into a barrel that you hope to use later for wine storage. Once acetic bacteria are in a barrel, that barrel is no longer useful for aging wine.

Many winemakers also make vinegar. I don't recommend it, but if you must, try to keep the vinegar separate from the winemaking facility, and never use the same equipment for wine and vinegar production or bottling.

Oxidation

Wine tends to oxidize when it is exposed to too much air, especially when SO_2 levels in the wine are insufficient. Oxidation turns wines slightly brown, which is especially noticeable in white wines. Oxidized wines take on a "cooked" smell and taste, much like a sherry. Once again, there's not much you can do with oxidized wine, but oxidation is easy to prevent if you use proper levels of SO_2, keep all containers topped up, and rack your wines gently.

Hydrogen Sulfide (H_2S)

Hydrogen sulfide is a compound formed near the end of alcoholic fermentation or shortly after fermentation while the wine is in contact with the lees. Even with the best of winemaking practices, you are likely to encounter this repugnant compound at some point in your career. It has a distinctive egg salad or rotten egg odor, and is detectable at very low concentrations. If you have a problem with hydrogen sulfide, you will know it.

The secret to dealing with H_2S is to identify and treat it as early as possible by splashing the wine and exposing it to air. Simply pour the wine from one clean bucket to another as demonstrated in my video. You will easily smell the hydrogen sulfide as the wine splashes back and forth from bucket to bucket. After a few minutes the smell should blow off. Pour the wine back into its original container, make sure that the container is topped up, adjust the SO_2, and the problem should be solved.

Early detection and treatment of H_2S problems is essential. Left alone, H_2S will compound into **mercapton** (cooked green bean smell) and **ethyl mercapton** (cooked asparagus smell). These are much more serious and require severe agents to correct the problem. If you have mercapton problems, get specific instructions from your local wine expert or call a winery lab service for instructions.

Molds and Yeasts

Molds can grow on the surface of wine, especially if the wine is stored in containers that are not completely full. In barrels and carboys where the wine has evaporated and come into contact with air, small whitish particles can form on the surface of the wine. Left unattended, these particles will multiply until they coat the entire surface of the wine.

If you encounter this problem, try to physically remove the particles from the surface with a clean paper towel or a syringe. Rack the wine into clean containers, make an SO_2 addition, and keep the containers filled and tightly sealed to minimize air contact. Then be sure to clean the infected container with chlorinated TSP or a 200 ppm SO_2 solution.

Moldy tastes or odors, the taste of wood or cork, and other uncharacteristic flavors are usually caused by poor sanitation. Use only clean equipment and sound barrels. Do not store wine in the presence of gasoline, pesticides, or any other strong smelling agents.

Too Much Oak

The amount of oak flavor in a wine is strictly a matter of personal taste. However, I think the fruit of the grape should be the most important component for any wine variety, and I prefer not to mask that character with too much oak. Limit the amount of time your wine spends in new oak barrels, as detailed in Chapter 9. Taste the wine regularly and often to assess how quickly oak is being imparted to the wine. Rack the wine when it has acquired the optimum amount of oak flavor.

If, the wine is too oaky, you can correct the problem by blending in some wine that has no oak whatsoever. This is another advantage in following the oak regimen detailed in Chapter 9.

Stuck Fermentations

Sooner or later every winemaker is confronted by a wine that won't finish fermenting. We call that a stuck fermentation. Sometimes a stuck fermentation defies explanation, but the three most common reasons are: 1) the grapes are too ripe and the resulting high alcohol is killing off the yeast; 2) the yeast is too weak to finish converting sugar to alcohol; or 3) the must lacks nutrients that are essential to the yeast.

In all three cases, it is best to keep the must warm, avoid SO_2 use, and try to finish out the fermentation. In the case of overripe grapes, adjusting the sugar as described in Chapter 5 is the easiest way to go. If it's too late to make that adjustment, you can make the wine in a late harvest style or you can try adding a different yeast strain that is more resistant to alcohol. Adding a different yeast strain is also effective in the case of weak yeasts that can't finish what they've started. Stuck fermentations are more common with native yeast fermentations than with prepared yeast cultures. Most winemakers will try adding yeast nutrients to any stuck fermentation, either as a separate step or in conjunction with one of the other remedies.

13
BOTTLING

The wine is ready to bottle when it is stable, when it has the desired amount of oak aging, when the pH, acidity, and SO_2 are at the desired levels, and when you decide that it tastes good.

Stability

First and foremost, wine stability means that the wine has finished primary fermentation, and that all available sugars have been converted to alcohol. In cases where you have intentionally left some residual sugar, the wine is not stable until all the yeast have been removed by filtering. Short of filtering, the best you can do is to keep the wine cold and maintain optimum SO_2 levels.

With those red and white wines you have inoculated with malolactic cultures, the malolactic fermentation must be completed. This can be measured using paper chromatography, as described in Chapter 6.

All wines should be cold stable so they will not throw tartrates. Cold stability is achieved by chilling the wines for a substantial period of time to allow the wine to form tartrates before bottling. White wines should be made protein stable through the use of bentonite as explained in Chapter 8.

Pre-bottling Measurements

Be sure to check the pH, TA, and SO_2 before bottling your wine. Adjust the SO_2 (as explained in Chapter 11) according to pH levels. Record the test data for future reference.

Most red wines are bottled with a total acidity range of .52–.65. White wines tend to be bottled with a slightly higher acidity range of .60–.75. Finished acidity in wines is largely a matter of taste. Taste the wines just before bottling. If you think they need more acid, try testing a small sample. Using your test data, determine how much you want to raise your wine's acidity. Take a small amount, make the proper acid addition, and then taste the acidulated wine against the same wine without the acid addition. Decide which you like the best, and proceed accordingly.

If your wine has too much acid, you can use **potassium carbonate** to lower the acidity. It is not difficult to use, but it does involve some additional work to achieve stability. Be sure to get complete instructions regarding lab trials, usage, and stabilization techniques from your supplier.

Blending

One of the great winemaking pleasures is blending. Often we make wines from a single vineyard. In that instance, we try to maintain the individual taste of the vineyard. Any blending we perform is to enhance interest and complexity of the finished wine.

Other wines are made by blending several different wines to make a complex, unique wine. Bordeaux-style blends using cabernet sauvignon, cabernet franc, and merlot provide a good example. In these situations, we blend for fruitiness, texture, mouth feel and finish. Whatever the style, blending is simple and fun. Basically, all you need is a graduated cylinder to measure small amounts of wine. Mix several sample blends using different amounts, pour them into glasses, and taste them.

Let's say you have some cabernet sauvignon and some merlot. Number five glasses. Pour straight cabernet into the first glass. Pour straight merlot into the fifth glass. Make a 50/50 mix of cabernet and merlot for the third glass. Try a 75/25 cabernet to merlot mix for the second glass. Try a 75/25 merlot to cabernet mix for the fourth glass. Now taste, and keep tasting until you decide which wine you prefer. You can refine your blends by using smaller percentage additions. For example, you may like a 90/10 mixture.

In situations where you are trying to maintain a single vineyard's character, you may prefer a wine with as little as a 2–3% addition from another vineyard. Blend and taste often. It is a great education for any winemaker. It is amazing how much effect even small amounts of wine can have on a blend.

Bottling

Now that the wine is ready to bottle, your key job is to minimize oxidation. Use new wine bottles or used bottles that have been washed, then rinsed with SO_2 solution, and finally rinsed with hot water. Simple gravity flow of the wine into the bottles helps reduce oxidation. Fill each bottle to allow a 1/4 inch space between the wine level and the inserted cork. I cover the entire bottling process in my video, *Making Wine at Home the Professional Way*.

Various corking devices, along with the corks themselves, are available at your local wine shop. Get the one that best suits you and your price range. **Remember, after corking wines, keep the bottles upright for a few days, and then turn them upside down so the wine is in contact with the corks.** Label each case with pertinent information such as wine type, vineyard, and date bottled.

Store the wines in a cool place away from sunlight and vibration. Be patient. Enjoy the wines as the spirit moves you.

GLOSSARY

Acetic acid — The main acid in vinegar.

Acetification — The formation of acetic acid (vinegar).

Aroma — Wine odors derived from grapes.

° Balling — A measurement of sugar in fermenting wine.

Bentonite — A type of clay used for heat stability.

Bound SO_2 — Sulfur dioxide that combines with other compounds.

Bouquet — Wine odors derived from processing, such as fermentation and oak aging.

° Brix — Measurement of sugar in juice.

Cap — The skins and pulp of crushed grapes that separate from the juice and float to the top during fermentation.

Carbon dioxide CO_2 — A gas formed during fermentation.

Carboy — A glass container

Cold stabilization	The removal of tartrates in wine to prevent precipitation in bottled wine.
Crusher	A device that breaks grapes skins to allow for juice extraction. Often removes grapes from their stems as well.
Deacidify	To reduce the total acidity in wine or juice.
Dry	A wine with no fermentable sugar.
Ethyl acetate	A compound smelling like nail polish remover.
Ethyl mercapton	A compound smelling like cooked asparagus.
Fermentation	The conversion of grape sugar by yeast to alcohol and carbon dioxide.
Fermenter	A container for fermenting wine.
Fermentation lock	A device that allows CO_2 to escape and prevents air from entering a container of wine.
Finish	The taste of wine that remains in the mouth after swallowing.
Free run	Juice or wine that flows from grapes without pressing.

Free SO$_2$	Sulfur dioxide actively available to protect wine.
Heat stabilization	The removal of excess proteins to prevent cloudiness in bottled wine.
Hydrogen sulfide	A compound smelling like rotten eggs.
Hydrometer	A device used for measuring sugar in juice or must.
Lactic acid	An organic acid produced from malic acid by bacteria.
Lactobacillus	A spoilage bacteria that can carry out malolactic fermentation.
Lees	Sediment from wine fermentation.
Leuconostoc oenus	The desired bacteria for carrying out malolactic fermentation.
Malic acid	One of the organic acids found in grapes.
Malolactic fermentation	Conversion of malic acid into lactic acid and CO$_2$ gas.
Mercapton	A compound smelling like cooked green beans.
Must	The crushed juice, skins, and pulp of grapes.

Oxidation	Browning and undesirable changes in a wine's flavor resulting from contact with oxygen.
pH	A measurement of hydrogen ions in solution used as an indicator for wine production.
Potassium carbonate	A compound that can reduce acidity when added to wine or juice.
ppm	Parts per million
Press	A device that extracts juice or wine from grapes.
Press juice	That fraction of juice or wine separated from the grapes by pressure.
Paper chromatography	A test to measure the progress of malolactic fermentation.
Punching down	Pushing the cap down into the juice during fermentation.
Racking	Moving juice or wine from one container to another.
Refractometer	A device to measure the sugar content of juice

Sulfur dioxide
SO_2
An antiseptic that inhibits the growth of bacteria, acts as an antioxidant, and can be used as a wine preservative and sanitizing agent.

Stuck fermentation
When a fermentation stops before all of the sugar is converted to alcohol.

Tannins
Compounds responsible for astringency and bitterness in wine, but also thought to contribute to a wine's ability to age.

Tartaric acid
The main organic acid found in grapes.

Tartrates
Crystals that can form naturally in chilled wine.

Topping up
Keeping containers of wine filled to the top to help prevent oxidation.

Total acidity (TA)
A measurement of the acid level in wine or juice.

Total SO_2
The concentration of SO_2 in juice or wine that includes both free and bound SO_2.

Yeast
Converts grape sugar to alcohol and CO_2 gas.

Order Form

Postal Orders: Send your check or money order to:
Wine Patrol Press
P.O. Box 228
Vineburg, CA 95487

Or fax (707) 938-9460

I need *Making Wine at Home the Professional Way with Lance Cutler.*

Please send _____ videos and _____ workbooks.

Name: _____

Address:_____

City: _____ State _____ Zip _____

Price: Videos are $29.95 each. Workbooks are $11.95 each, but you can purchase the video and workbook together for $35.95, a savings of $5.95.

Shipping: $3.00 for the first book or video, and $0.75 for each additional book or video in the same package.

Sales tax: Please add 7.25% for items shipped to a California address.

Amount enclosed _____

Also from **Wine Patrol Press**

Cold Surveillance: The Jake Lorenzo Columns
by Jake Lorenzo

Cold Surveillance is the best book about wine that I've read in years.
Jerry Henry
***WWL Radio*, New Orleans**

In the wonderful, but complex world of wine, there is nobody like Jake Lorenzo. Nobody. He is our Henry Miller, our Paul Gaugin, our Robin Williams.
Bob Sessions
Hanzell Vineyards

Ever outrageous, ever exhilarating, ever for freedom without distinction, ever for life at its most intense.
Gerald Asher
Gourmet Magazine

Pull up a chair, open a bottle, and enter Jake's world. A bottle of wine will never be the same.

Order Now!

Cold Surveillance **by Jake Lorenzo**
only $9.95 (plus $3.00 for shipping and handling)